I0881199

WORLD OF WORK

HUMAN SERVICES

Exploring Career Pathways

Diane Lindsey Reeves

Created and produced by
Bright Futures Press, Cary, North Carolina
www.brightfuturespress.com

Published by
Cherry Lake Publishing, Ann Arbor, Michigan
www.cherrylakepublishing.com

Photo Credits: Cover, Beautyline; page 7, Olimpik, Phonlamai Photo, Alexander Raths, Roman Rybaleov, michaeljung, sakhorn, bikeridelondon, Iakov Filimonor; page 8, Olimpik; page 10, Phonlamai Photo; page 12, Alexander Raths; page 14, Roman Rybaleov; page 16, michaeljung; page 18, sakhorn; page 20, bikeridelondon; page 22, Iakov Filimonor, page 24, Rawpizel.com.

Library of Congress Cataloging-in-Publication Date

CIP data has been filed and is available at catalog.loc.gov.

Printed in the United States of America.

TABLE OF CONTENTS

HELLO WORLD OF WORK

This is you.

Right now, your job is to go to school and learn all you can.

This is the world of work.

It's where people earn a living, find purpose in their lives, and make the world a better place.

Sooner or later, you'll have to find your way from

HERE to THERE.

To get started, take all the jobs in the incredibly enormous world of work and organize them into an imaginary pile. It's a big pile, isn't it? It would be pretty tricky to find the perfect job for you among so many options.

No worries!

Some very smart career experts have made it easier to figure out. They sorted jobs and industries into groups by the types of skills and products they share. These groups are called career clusters. They provide pathways that will make it easier for you to find career options that match your interests.

- Architecture & Construction
- Arts & Communication
- Business & Administration
- Education & Training
- Finance
- Food & Natural Resources
- Government
- Health Sciences
- Hospitality & Tourism
- Human Services
- Information Technology
- Law & Public Safety
- Manufacturing
- Marketing, Sales & Service
- Science, Technology, Engineering & Mathematics (STEM)
- Transportation

Good thing you are still a kid.

You have lots of time to explore ideas and imagine yourself doing all kinds of amazing things. The **World of Work** (WoW for short) series of books will help you get started.

TAKE A HIKE!

There are 16 career pathways waiting for you to explore. The only question is: Which one should you explore first?

Is **Human Services** a good path for you to start exploring career ideas? There is a lot to like about this pathway. These professionals take care of other people's needs in good times and bad. They provide support services and programs that enrich families and communities. Their work makes the world a better place.

See if any of the following questions grab your interest.

WOULD YOU ENJOY showing a new kid around your school, organizing a neighborhood food drive, or being a peer mediator?

CAN YOU IMAGINE someday working at an elder care center, fitness center, or mental health center?

ARE YOU CURIOUS ABOUT what elder care center directors, hairstylists, personal trainers, psychologists, or religious leaders do?

If so, it's time to take a hike! Keep reading to see what kinds of opportunities you can discover along the Human Services pathway.

But wait!

What if you don't think you'll like this pathway?

You have two choices.

You could keep reading, to find out more than you already know. You might be surprised to learn how many amazing careers you'll find along this path.

OR

Turn to page 27 to get ideas about other WoW pathways.

WoW Up Close

They provide services for people young, old, and in between. They meet many kinds of physical, emotional, mental, and spiritual needs. They help people cope with problems, trauma, and disaster. These are just some of the important jobs found along the Human Services pathway.

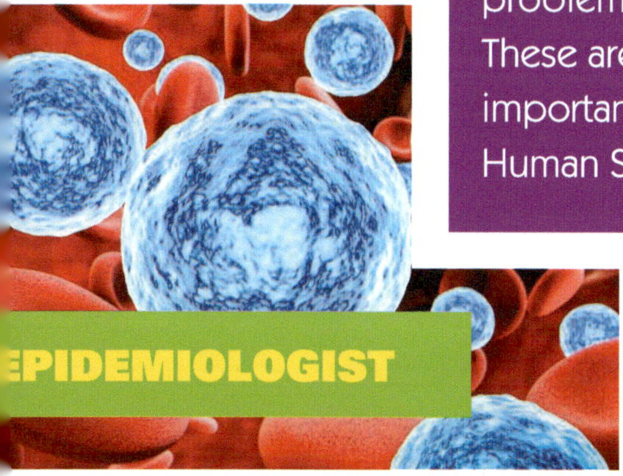

CHILD PSYCHOLOGIST

Everyone has problems, even kids. Sometimes the problems get so big that children need help dealing with them. **Child psychologists** work with individual children to identify problems and **diagnose** conditions. They help by providing counseling, **therapy**, and other support.

Some child psychologists work with children with emotional problems. Perhaps the child is dealing with depression or anxiety. Sometimes a child needs extra help after going through a bad experience like losing a parent or being abused. In these cases, a child psychologist might meet with the child to provide therapy over a period of time. Depending on the problem, the psychologist might refer the child to other services or to a doctor for medication.

Other child psychologists specialize in working with children who have learning disabilities or developmental issues such as **autism**. In these situations, they test and **evaluate** the child and make recommendations for treatment.

It takes a college degree to get started as a child psychologist. The more education a child psychologist has, the more opportunities there are to work in schools, colleges, hospitals, government, and private practice. Future child psychologists can start now by taking lots of science classes in school.

Check It Out!

Explore all kinds of issues about kids' health at

- http://kidshealth.org/en/kids

Start Now!

- Child psychologists need to be good listeners, so practice paying attention in class and when friends talk to you.
- Be on the lookout for ways you can help and show kindness to your friends and family.
- Find out if your school has a peer mediation program and get involved.

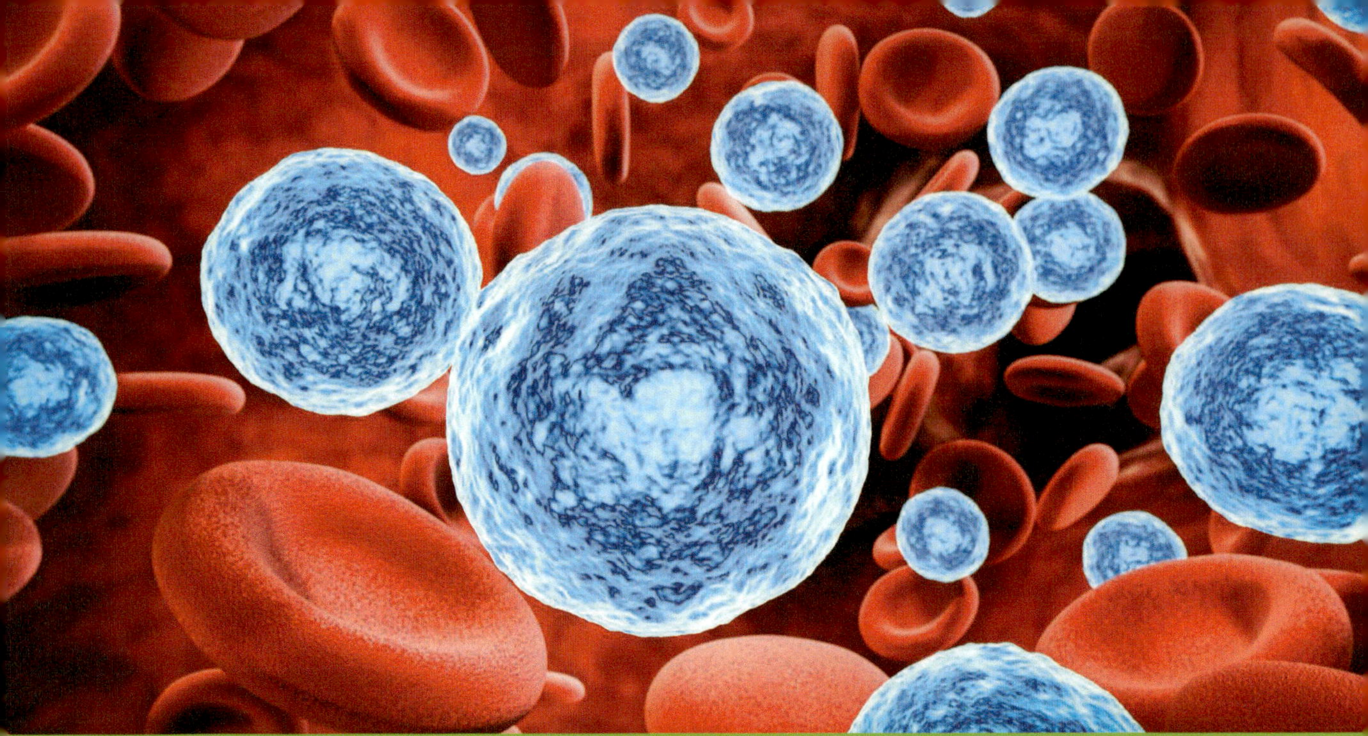

EPIDEMIOLOGIST

Epidemiologists are disease detectives. As an example, imagine that lots of kids in your school started getting icky rashes from head to toe. It wasn't hives. It wasn't measles. Doctors couldn't figure out what it was or why so many students were getting it.

They did know that it was highly **contagious** and that they had to do something to stop the outbreak. That's when they would call in epidemiologists from the public health department to investigate.

This is what happens when diseases start to spread among people in a specific place. It could be a school, a community, or a certain place in the world. These outbreaks are called **epidemics**. If not stopped, an epidemic can cause major health problems. In recent years, there was an **Ebola** epidemic in West Africa. This deadly disease spread quickly from village to village. It was so contagious that it soon spread to other countries. Thousands of people died before doctors and scientists were able to contain the outbreak and develop a vaccine.

Learning how to investigate epidemics requires at least a master's degree from college. Epidemiologists must have a strong background in both math and science. The job requires lots of research, working with data, and analyzing information that provides clues about how to stop the spread of a disease.

Check It Out!

Solve some online epidemics at

- http://www.diseasedetectives.org
- http://www.mclph.umn.edu/watersedge

Start Now!

- Go online to see what you can find out about John Snow, the "father" of epidemiology.
- Make a brochure that gives tips on how to avoid passing a common cold on to other people.
- Pick a common contagious disease like the flu, measles or tuberculosis and find out all you can about its symptoms and cures.

GERIATRIC CASE MANAGER

A **geriatric case manager** is part social worker, part nurse, and part psychologist. They are experts in understanding the needs of elderly people. It is the case managers' job to determine what they need and plan ways to help them. They also speak out, or **advocate**, for older people.

As people age, they face a variety of challenges. They may experience health problems that make them unable to care for themselves. They may need to move from a family home into a smaller home or into an facility where they can receive care. They sometimes face financial problems when they are no longer able to work. A person's mate may die. These are big problems that become even bigger when advanced age makes it difficult or impossible for a person to deal with them on their own.

Geriatric case managers step in to provide services that help older people and their families. They have a college degree in an aging life care field or geriatrics. They are also licensed to provide the kinds of services older people need to enjoy a better quality of life.

By the year 2050, the number of Americans who are over the age of 65 is supposed to be twice as high as it was in 2012. That means there will be lots of elderly people and lots of opportunity for others to provide services for them.

Check It Out!

Go online to explore "elder care options" in your hometown.

Start Now!

- Volunteer to read and play games with senior citizens at a local assisted living facility.
- Ask your grandparents to share stories about what their lives were like when they were your age.

HAIRSTYLIST

When people have bad hair days, they go to a **hairstylist** for help! Hairstylists shampoo, cut, color, and style hair to get men, women, and children looking their best. Hair grows at an average of a half inch each month. Unless they want to look like Rapunzel (the fairy tale character whose hair grew to be 70 feet long), most people need to visit a hairstylist from time to time.

Of course, not everyone has hair. But that's another story!

Hairstylists must complete a special training program, get experience, and pass a written and practical skills exam in order to be licensed to work as a stylist. They do this by either completing a training program at a cosmetology school or working as an apprentice for a licensed stylist. Either way, beginning stylists learn the tricks of the trade under the watchful eye of someone with lots of experience. This process involves an average of 1,500 hours of practice and usually takes one to two years to complete.

Once hairstylists are licensed, they work in a salon, hotel, or resort and build up a list of **clientele** who trust them to take scissors to their hair. Successful stylists build relationships with customers that keep them coming back for services time and time again. Stylists also keep up with the latest trends and techniques so they can keep their customers looking good.

Check It Out!

See how you like the latest looks in hair

- http://pantene.com/en-us/hairstyles
- http://www.thehairstyler.com
- http://www.latest-hairstyles.com

Start Now!

- Experiment with different ways to style your own hair (preferably without using scissors!).
- Clip pictures out of magazines of hairstyles that you like, to make your own style catalog.
- Next time you get your hair done, ask your stylist to tell you about what his or her job is like.

PERSONAL TRAINER

Personal trainers are physical fitness experts. They work with individuals or groups to get them into tip-top physical shape. Their job is to work with clients to set fitness goals, create a plan of action, and then motivate each client to work it, work it, work it!

People have different reasons for working out. It may be to lose weight or look better. It may be to recover from an injury or illness, or it may be to prevent injuries and illnesses. No matter the reason, it is a good idea for people to get—and stay—in shape.

People tend to have unique workout styles and preferences. Some people like to work really hard—to the limits of their endurance. They give their best results to a personal trainer who lays down the law and barks out orders. Others work better with more gentle encouragement and rewards. It's up to the personal trainer to determine the best ways to train and motivate each client. It's like having your own personal fitness coach!

Some trainers have college degrees in a health or fitness field. Others work toward certification in a specific area of fitness, such as water, weightlifting, yoga, or nutrition.

The first qualification for being a personal trainer is being in good shape. Practicing healthy habits in fitness and nutrition sets a good example for clients. This is one profession where it is especially important to practice what you preach!

Check It Out!

Find out more about making healthy choices at

- https://letsmove.obamawhitehouse.archives.gov
- http://bit.ly/AstronautFit
- http://www.kidnetic.com

Start Now!

- Set a new fitness goal and make a chart to keep track of your progress.
- Put together a workout routine and teach it to a friend or sibling.
- Make a chart with ideas for replacing junk food snacks, like candy and soda, with healthy choices.

PROBATION OFFICER

When people are convicted of a crime, they are often sent to prison. After they have served some time, they might try to prove to a parole board that they are ready to be a good citizen again. If they can do this, they are set free—with a catch.

They are released under the supervision of a probation officer who will keep a close watch over them for a set period of time (called probation) to make sure they are staying out of trouble.

You may think your parents are strict when you get in trouble, but probation officers are probably even stricter! They have two main goals. One is to make sure their clients do not commit any new crimes. The second is to give their clients a second chance to build a good life.

To do this, they have to keep close watch on what their clients are doing, where they are going, and who they are hanging out with. They have regular meetings with the clients and the clients' family. They might conduct drug tests and refer clients to various treatment programs. They connect clients with resources to get training and find jobs.

There is a lot at stake, and clients who mess up may get sent back to prison. That's why probation officers need to know a lot about how to deal with people. They have to be problem solvers, tough, and fair.

Check It Out!

Get acquainted with McGruff the Crime Dog at

- http://bit.ly/McGruff1
- http://bit.ly/McGruff2

Start Now!

- Find out if your school has a DARE (Drug Abuse Resistance Education) program and if there are ways you can get involved.
- Thank a police officer or first responder for doing what they do to keep your community safe.
- Make a poster to encourage fellow students to obey the law and stay out of trouble.

RELIGIOUS LEADER

What do pastors, priests, rabbis, and imams all share in common? They are **religious leaders** who guide others in matters of religious faith. They lead services and perform special functions like weddings, baptisms, or funerals.

Teaching and delivering **sermons** is a big part of the job for many religious leaders. This requires hours of research and preparation each week. It also requires excellent public speaking skills to convey information in ways that cause people to listen and understand.

Religious leaders may be involved in the management of the facilities where they hold their worship services. Taking good care of the places where people worship shows a special kind of respect for the reason people gather there. They are also accountable for the funds of the church, temple, or mosque.

A very important part of the work is looking out for the needs of the people who belong to the congregation. Religious leaders typically spend a good deal of time counseling members about problems, visiting those who are sick, and comforting those who have lost loved ones.

Religious leaders are expected to lead by example. They truly care about the members of their congregation and about doing good in the communities where they serve.

Check It Out!

Find out more about famous religious leaders at

http://bit.ly/FamousLeaders

Start Now!

- Visit a local place of worship with your family.
- Volunteer to help teach religious education classes for younger children at your place of worship.
- Talk with a friend or family member about what you believe and why you believe it.

SOCIAL WORKER

Social workers help children and families solve and cope with everyday problems. Wherever people with problems are found, you are likely to find social workers. This includes places like mental health clinics, schools, drug rehabilitation centers, child welfare agencies, hospitals, and community development groups. Or they have might have a private practice.

Social workers can't solve every problem for every person, so they tend to specialize in specific areas of need. Some work with children. This might involve removing children from abusive home situations and placing them with foster families or adoptive parents. Some social workers work with people who have **substance abuse** problems. They provide counseling, therapy, and other services.

Those social workers who work in hospitals may serve as a patient advocate. It is their job to help patients get the care and treatment they need. Still other social workers help homeless people get back on their feet.

Social workers must earn a master's degree in social work. After they get experience and pass a special exam, they can be licensed to help people in need. Social workers tend to encounter people who are going through some of the toughest times of their lives. The work can be difficult and, at times, heartbreaking. Even so, it is rewarding work, and there is no doubt that social workers make a difference in the lives of those they help.

Check It Out!

Find out more about the different types of social work at

- http://bit.ly/SocWork1
- http://bit.ly/SocWork2

Start Now!

- Talk to your parents about volunteering as a family to help others through your place of worship or community center.
- Make a habit of treating others with kindness and respect.
- Learn all you can about an issue that you care about, like substance abuse, homelessness, or adoption.

Account executive • Activities director • Addictions counselor • Aesthetician • Afterschool program director • Apartment manager • Assessment services manager • Assisted living administrator • Author • Barber • Behavioral analyst • Bereavement counselor • Call center representative • Care advocate • Career counselor • Case manager • Certified nursing assistant • Child care center director • Child care provider • **CHILD PSYCHOLOGIST** • Choir director • City planner • Clinical services director • Clinical social worker • Community health consultant • Conductor • Counselor • Customer service representative

WoW Big List

Take a look at some of the different kinds of jobs people do in the Human Services pathway. **WoW!**

Some of these job titles will be familiar to you. Others will be so unfamiliar that you will scratch your head and say "huh?"

• District sales manager • Elder care provider • Environmental program manager • **EPIDEMIOLOGIST** • Extension agent • Family and consumer sciences teacher • Fashion designer • Fitness instructor • **GERIATRIC CASE MANAGER** • Gerontologist • **HAIRSTYLIST** • Home health care aide • Hospice worker • Housing specialist • Industrial psychologist • Interpreter • Job coach • Lab manager • Leasing manager •

Legislator • Literacy specialist • Makeup artist • Marketing director • Marriage and family therapist • Massage therapist • Mathematician • Medicaid analyst • Mortician • Music director • Music therapist • Nail technician • Nanny • Nurse • Organizational psychologist • Parole officer • **PERSONAL TRAINER** • Physician • Physician's assistant • Preschool director • Preschool teacher • **PROBATION OFFICER** • Product developer • Property manager • Psychologist • Public health educator • Public relations specialist • Recreation supervisor • Rehabilitation counselor • Religious education director •

Find a job title that makes you curious. Type the name of the job into your favorite Internet search engine and find out more about the people who have that job.

1. What do they do?
2. Where do they work?
3. How much training do they need to do this job?

RELIGIOUS LEADER • Residential counselor • Retail loss prevention officer • Retail store manager • Sales representative • Salon manager • School psychologist • **SOCIAL WORKER** • Sociologist • Songwriter • Substance abuse counselor • Summer camp director •Surgeon • Tailor • Teen program manager • Therapist • Translator • Victim advocate • Workforce advisor • Worship arts leader • Youth director

TAKE YOUR PICK

	Put stars next to your 3 favorite career ideas	Put an X next to the career idea you like the least	Put a question mark next to the career idea you want to learn more about
Child psychologist			
Epidemiologist			
Geriatric case manager			
Hairstylist			
Personal trainer			
Probation officer			
Religious leader			
Social worker			

What do you like most about these careers?	What is it about this career that doesn't appeal to you?	What do you want to learn about this career? Where can you find answers?

Which Big Wow List ideas are you curious about?

Please do **NOT** write in this book if it doesn't belong to you. You can download a copy of this activity online at www.brightfuturespress.com/teacher-guides.

EXPLORE SOME MORE

The Human Services pathway is only one of 16 career pathways that hold exciting options for your future. Take a look at the other 15 to figure out where to start exploring next.

Architecture & Construction

WOULD YOU ENJOY making things with LEGOs™, building a treehouse or birdhouse, or designing the world's best skate park?

CAN YOU IMAGINE someday working at a construction site, a design firm, or a building company?

ARE YOU CURIOUS ABOUT what civil engineers, demolition technicians, heavy-equipment operators, landscape architects, or urban planners do?

Arts & Communication

WOULD YOU ENJOY drawing your own cartoons, using your smartphone to make a movie, or writing articles for the student newspaper?

CAN YOU IMAGINE someday working at a Hollywood movie studio, a publishing company, or a television news station?

ARE YOU CURIOUS ABOUT what actors, bloggers, graphic designers, museum curators, or writers do?

Business & Administration

WOULD YOU ENJOY playing Monopoly, being the boss of your favorite club or team, or starting your own business?

CAN YOU IMAGINE someday working at a big corporate headquarters, government agency, or international business center?

ARE YOU CURIOUS ABOUT what brand managers, chief executive officers, e-commerce analysts, entrepreneurs, or purchasing agents do?

Education & Training

WOULD YOU ENJOY babysitting, teaching your grandparents how to use a computer, or running a summer camp for neighbor kids in your backyard?

CAN YOU IMAGINE someday working at a college counseling center, corporate training center, or school?

ARE YOU CURIOUS ABOUT what animal trainers, coaches, college professors, guidance counselors, or principals do?

Finance

WOULD YOU ENJOY earning and saving money, being the class treasurer, or playing the stock market game?

CAN YOU IMAGINE someday working at an accounting firm, bank, or Wall Street stock exchange?

ARE YOU CURIOUS ABOUT what accountants, bankers, fraud investigators, property managers, or stockbrokers do?

Food & Natural Resources

WOULD YOU ENJOY exploring nature, growing your own garden, or setting up a recycling center at your school?

CAN YOU IMAGINE someday working at a national park, raising crops in a city farm, or studying food in a laboratory?

ARE YOU CURIOUS ABOUT what landscape architects, chefs, food scientists, environmental engineers, or forest rangers do?

Government

WOULD YOU ENJOY reading about U.S. presidents, running for student council, or helping a favorite candidate win an election?

CAN YOU IMAGINE someday working at a chamber of commerce, government agency, or law firm?

ARE YOU CURIOUS about what mayors, customs agents, federal special agents, intelligence analysts, or politicians do?

Health Sciences

WOULD YOU ENJOY nursing a sick pet back to health, dissecting animals in a science lab, or helping the school coach run a sports clinic?

CAN YOU IMAGINE someday working at a dental office, hospital, or veterinary clinic?

ARE YOU CURIOUS ABOUT what art therapists, doctors, dentists, pharmacists, and veterinarians do?

Hospitality & Tourism

WOULD YOU ENJOY traveling, sightseeing, or meeting people from other countries?

CAN YOU IMAGINE someday working at a convention center, resort, or travel agency?

ARE YOU CURIOUS ABOUT what convention planners, golf pros, tour guides, resort managers, or wedding planners do?

Information Technology

WOULD YOU ENJOY creating your own video game, setting up a Web site, or building your own computer?

CAN YOU IMAGINE someday working at an information technology start-up company, software design firm, or research and development laboratory?

ARE YOU CURIOUS ABOUT what artificial intelligence scientists, big data analysts, computer forensic investigators, software engineers, or video game designers do?

Law & Public Safety

WOULD YOU ENJOY working on the school safety patrol, participating in a mock court trial at school, or coming up with a fire escape plan for your home?

CAN YOU IMAGINE someday working at a cyber security company, fire station, police department, or prison?

ARE YOU CURIOUS ABOUT what animal control officers, coroners, detectives, firefighters, or park rangers do?

Manufacturing

WOULD YOU ENJOY figuring out how things are made, competing in a robot-building contest, or putting model airplanes together?

CAN YOU IMAGINE someday working at a high-tech manufacturing plant, engineering firm, or global logistics company?

ARE YOU CURIOUS ABOUT what chemical engineers, industrial designers, supply chain managers, robotics technologists, or welders do?

Marketing, Sales & Service

WOULD YOU ENJOY keeping up with the latest fashion trends, picking favorite TV commercials during Super Bowl games, or making posters for a favorite school club?

CAN YOU IMAGINE someday working at an advertising agency, corporate marketing department, or retail store?

ARE YOU CURIOUS ABOUT what creative directors, market researchers, media buyers, retail store managers, and social media consultants do?

Science, Technology, Engineering & Mathematics (STEM)

WOULD YOU ENJOY concocting experiments in a science lab, trying out the latest smartphone, or taking advanced math classes?

CAN YOU IMAGINE someday working in a science laboratory, engineering firm, or research and development center?

ARE YOU CURIOUS ABOUT what aeronautical engineers, ecologists, statisticians, oceanographers, or zoologists do?

Transportation

WOULD YOU ENJOY taking pilot or sailing lessons, watching a NASA rocket launch, or helping out in the school carpool lane?

CAN YOU IMAGINE someday working at an airport, mass transit system, or shipping port?

ARE YOU CURIOUS ABOUT what air traffic controllers, flight attendants, logistics planners, surveyors, and traffic engineers do?

MY WoW

I am here.

Name

Grade

School

Who I am.

Make a word collage! Use 5 adjectives to form a picture that describes who you are.

Where I'm going.

The next career pathway I want to explore is

Some things I need to learn first to succeed.

1

2

3

To get here.

Please do **NOT** write in this book if it doesn't belong to you. You can download a copy of this activity online at www.brightfuturespress.com/teacher-guides.

GLOSSARY

advocate
person who supports or speaks out on behalf of a person, an idea, or a plan

apprentice
someone who learns a skill by working with an expert

autism
a condition that causes someone to have trouble learning, communicating, and forming relationships with people

child psychologist
person who helps children deal with emotional, behavioral, and development problems

clientele
regular customers who return to the same shop or service provider

contagious
spread by direct or indirect contact with an infected person or animal

diagnose
to determine what disease or problem a patient is suffering from

Ebola
an infectious and frequently fatal disease marked by fever and severe internal bleeding

epidemics
infectious diseases present in a large number of people at the same time

epidemiologist
scientist who studies diseases within populations of people

evaluate
to decide the condition of something by thinking carefully about it

geriatric case manager
person who is trained to plan and provide services for the elderly and their families

geriatrics
the study of the health and care of very old people

hairstylist
person who shampoos, cuts, colors, and styles other people's hair

outbreak
sudden start and spread of something unpleasant, such as a contagious disease

parole
the early release of a prisoner, usually for good behavior, on the condition that the person continues to obey the law

personal trainer
person who helps others achieve fitness goals

probation
period of time during which a person who has committed a crime is not kept in prison but is allowed to go free under the close supervision of a probation officer

probation officer
person who is appointed to supervise criminal offenders who are on probation

religious leader
person who guides others in matters of faith

sermons
speeches given during religious services

social worker
person who helps other people solve problems through advocacy, education, advice, and other support

substance abuse
misuse of something considered to harmful, such as drugs or alcohol

therapy
treatment for an illness, injury, disability, or psychological problem

INDEX

*** Refers to the Web page sources**

About the Author

Diane Lindsey Reeves is the author of lots of children's books. She has written several original PEANUTS stories (published by Regnery Kids and Sourcebooks). She is especially curious about what people do and likes to write books that get kids thinking about all the cool things they can be when they grow up. She lives in Cary, North Carolina, and her favorite thing to do is play with her grandkids—Conrad, Evan, Reid, and Hollis Grace.